To Ken, with appreciation and expectations of great things to come. Stay in touch!

Kevin O'Brien

5/19/99